AFFIRMATIONS
Living Day by Day

AFFIRMATIONS

Living Day by Day

Copyright © 1990 Antioch Publishing Company
Yellow Springs, Ohio 45387
ISBN 0-89954-511-4

CONTENTS

❈LETTING GOD HELP❈

THOUGHTS FOR TODAY

-It is better to recognize my problems than to go on denying them and denying reality.

-It is a victory, not a failure, to admit that I cannot control my problems. I cannot control everything that happens in life— just as I cannot do everything and do it alone.

-It is a positive step to "let go and let God" help me with my problems. If I commit my life to a Higher Power, it will lead me to serenity.

-It is helpful to call to mind this old proverb: The marksman hits the target partly by pulling, partly by letting go. The boatsman reaches the landing partly by pulling, partly by letting go.

GOD IS AWAKE

Have courage for the great sorrows of life and patience for the small ones; and when you have laboriously accomplished your daily task, go to sleep in peace. God is awake.

—Victor Hugo

IF WE LOOK UP

In our whole life melody the music is broken off here and there by rests, and we foolishly think we have come to the end of time. God sends a time of forced leisure, a time of sickness and disappointed plans, and makes a sudden pause in the hymns of our lives, and we lament that our voice must be silent and our part missing in the music which ever goes up to the ear of our Creator. Not without design does God write the music of our lives. Be it ours to learn the time and not be dismayed at the rests. If we look up, God will beat the time for us.

—John Ruskin

THE DIFFERENCE

I got up early one morning
And rushed right into the day;
I had so much to accomplish
That I didn't have time to pray.
Problems just tumbled about me,
And heavier came each task;
"Why doesn't God help me?"
I wondered.
He answered, "You didn't ask."
I wanted to see joy and beauty,
But the day toiled on gray and bleak;
I wondered why God didn't show me.
He said, "But you didn't seek."
I tried to come into God's presence;
I used all my keys in the lock.
God gently and lovingly chided,
"My child, you didn't knock."
I woke up early this morning,
And paused before entering the day;
I had so much to accomplish
That I had to take time to pray.

—Author Unknown

TRUST IN GOD

The person who has a firm trust in the
Supreme Being is powerful in his power,
wise by his wisdom, happy by his
happiness.

—Joseph Addison

Happiness is neither within us only, or
without us; it is the union of ourselves with
God.

—Blaise Pascal

Trust in the Lord with all your heart and
lean not on your own understanding...

Proverbs 3:5 (NIV)

...those who hope in the Lord will renew
their strength. They will soar on wings like
eagles; they will run and not grow weary,
they will walk and not be faint.

Isaiah 40:31 (NIV)

YOU ARE NOT ALONE

Remember never to say that you are alone,
for you are not alone; God is within, and
your genius is within...

—Epictetus

Just as there comes a warm sunbeam into
every cottage window, so comes a love-
beam of God's care and pity for every
separate need.

—Nathaniel Hawthorne

❧BEING TRUE TO YOURSELF❧

THOUGHTS FOR TODAY

-Knowing myself is an important part of growth and change. It is essential to take an honest look at myself—my good qualities, my faults, my true feelings, including the guilt, the anger, and the pain.

-Facing my feelings can help get rid of the useless burdens I've been carrying around that only weigh me down.

-It is necessary to admit what I've done wrong— to myself, to God, and to others— and to ask forgiveness and also to forgive.

-It is better to communicate honestly about my thoughts and feelings, both with myself and others, especially when I need to say "no."

TO THINE OWN SELF BE TRUE

Know thyself.
—Socrates

This above all: to thine own self be true,
And it must follow, as the night the day,
Thou canst not then be false to any man.
—William Shakespeare

Resolve to be thyself; and know that he
Who finds himself, loses his misery.
—Matthew Arnold

To be what we are, and to become what we
are capable of becoming, is the only end of
life.
—Robert Louis Stevenson

What you are must always displease, if
you would attain to that which you are not.
—St. Augustine

THE COURAGE TO COMMUNICATE

Let us say what we feel, and feel what we say; let speech harmonize with life.

—Seneca

One must have the courage to say "no," even at the risk of displeasing others.

—Fritz Künkel

❧ LOVING YOURSELF ❧

THOUGHTS FOR TODAY

-It is healthy to accept myself as I am, to like myself, and to love myself. It is okay for me to accept a compliment or praise.

-Because I am just as deserving and worthy as anyone else, I may treat myself as well as I treat others, live my own life, and enjoy my life.

-There is a difference between being unselfish and being a martyr or a victim. There is a time for putting myself first so that I may take care of myself and my needs.

FIRST LEARN TO LOVE YOURSELF

First learn to love yourself, and then you can love me.

—St. Bernard of Clairvaux

Above all things, reverence yourself.

—Pythagoras

All must respect those who respect themselves.

—Benjamin Disraeli

If you want to be respected by others, the great thing is to respect yourself.

—Fyodor Dostoyevski

Do not have too great care about being useful to others, but be greatly concerned about being useful to yourself.

—Giles of Assisi

❧Trusting Yourself❧

THOUGHTS FOR TODAY

-To make my life better, I must be responsible for myself. I cannot be responsible for others and they cannot be responsible for me.

-Being responsible means that I have faith in myself and rely on myself. I trust myself; I trust God; I trust others. I believe that my judgement and decisions are trustworthy.

-My happiness does not depend on other people, but on myself. It does not depend on another's need for me or on my need for another.

-Not being responsible for others' lives does not mean that I don't care or that God doesn't want me to help. It means that I cannot take care of another's needs to the point of harming myself.

WINGS

Be like the bird
That, pausing in her flight
Awhile on boughs too slight,
Feels them give way
Beneath her and yet sings,
Knowing that she hath wings.
—*Victor Hugo*

BELIEVING IN YOURSELF

Trust thyself: every heart vibrates to that iron string.

—*Ralph Waldo Emerson*

Life is not easy for any of us. But what of that? We must have perseverance and above all confidence in ourselves. We must believe that we are gifted for something, and that this thing, at whatever cost, must be attained.

—*Madame Curie*

Look well into thyself; there is a source of strength which will always spring up if thou wilt always look there.

—*Marcus Aurelius*

I am bigger than anything that can happen to me.

—*C. F. Lummis*

Nothing happens to anybody which he is not fitted by nature to bear.

—*Marcus Aurelius*

Self-reliance and self-respect are about as valuable commodities as we can carry in our pack through life.

—*Luther Burbank*

I am the master of my fate;
I am the captain of my soul.

—*W. E. Henley*

No bird soars too high, if he soars with his own wings.

—*William Blake*

Believe that life is worth living and your belief will create the fact. Be not afraid to live.

—*William James*

They can conquer who believe they can.
—*Ralph Waldo Emerson*

Our belief at the beginning of a doubtful undertaking is the one thing that insures the successful outcome of our venture.
—*William James*

It is by believing in roses that one brings them to bloom.

—French Proverb

All things are possible to one who believes.

—St. Bernard of Clairvaux

"I tell you the truth, if you have faith as small as a mustard seed, you can say to this mountain, 'Move from here to there' and it will move. Nothing will be impossible for you."

Matthew 17:20,21 (NIV)

GOD TRUSTS YOU

God gives every bird its food, but He does not throw it into the nest.

—Josiah Holland

To the man who himself strives earnestly, God also lends a helping hand.

—Aeschylus

Help yourself, and Heaven will help you.

—Jean de La Fontaine

Heaven never helps the man who will not act.

—Sophocles

For God did not give us a spirit of timidity, but a spirit of power, of love and of self-discipline.

2 Timothy 1:7 (NIV)

God has delivered yourself to your care, and says: I had no one fitter to trust than you. Preserve this person for Me such as he is by nature: modest, beautiful, faithful, noble, tranquil.

—Epictetus

I can do everything through Him who gives me strength.

Philippians 4:13 (NIV)

HAPPINESS LIES WITHIN

Most folks are about as happy as they
make up their minds to be.

—Abraham Lincoln

Happiness depends upon ourselves.

—Aristotle

The man who makes everything that leads
to happiness depend upon himself, and not
upon other men, has adopted the very best
plan for living happily.

—Plato

When you see a person seeking happiness
outside himself, you can be sure he has
never found it.

—Lincicome

❖LEARNING TO CHANGE❖

THOUGHTS FOR TODAY

-In order to change, I must first be willing to change, then take the necessary action to change.

-Merely reacting—and overreacting—to the lives and actions of others is not living. Instead of being blown about like paper in the wind, I must act and so live my own life.

-Setting goals, even small ones, is a first step to positive change and growth. Although I cannot control every single thing in life, it is possible to make plans. What is important is to try. If things don't work out, I will accept it, try again, or find an alternative solution.

BEGINNINGS

First say to yourself what you would be;
and then do what you have to do.
>—*Ralph Waldo Emerson*

Fear not that thy life shall come to an end,
but rather fear that it shall never have a
beginning.
>—*John Henry Newman*

Every day we ought to renew our purpose,
saying to ourselves: This day let us make a
sound beginning...
>—*Thomas à Kempis*

In His great mercy He has given us new
birth into a living hope through the
resurrection of Jesus Christ...
>*1 Peter 1:3 (NIV)*

CHANGING

Today is not yesterday. We ourselves
change... Change, indeed, is painful, yet
ever needful; and if memory have its force
and worth, so also has hope.
—Thomas Carlyle

Very often a change of self is needed more
than a change of scene.
—Arthur C. Benson

Time was, I shrank from what was right,
From fear of what was wrong;
I would not brave the sacred fight,
Because the foe was strong.
But now I cast that finer sense
And sorer shame aside;
Such dread of sin was indolence,
Such aim at Heaven was pride.
—John Henry Newman

A FREE MIND

I call that mind free which is not passively framed by outward circumstances, which is not swept away by the torrent of events, which is not the creature of accidental impulse, but which bends events to its own improvement, and acts from an inward spring, from immutable principles which it has deliberately espoused.

—*W. E. Channing*

WE MUST SAIL

To reach the port of Heaven we must sail, sometimes with the wind and sometimes against it—but we must sail, not drift or lie at anchor.

—Oliver Wendell Holmes

I will be...no longer a dreamer among shadows. Henceforth be mine a life of action and reality! I will work in my own sphere, nor wish it other than it is. This alone is health and happiness.

—Henry Wadsworth Longfellow

I find the great thing in this world is not so much where we stand, as in what direction we are moving.

—Oliver Wendell Holmes

OUR LIFE

To live is not merely to breathe; it is to act;
it is to make use...of all those parts of
ourselves which give us the feeling of
existence. The man who has lived longest
is not the man who has counted most
years, but he who has enjoyed life most.

—Jean-Jacques Rousseau

Our life is a gift from God. What we do
with that life is our gift to God.

—Author Unknown

The time God allots to each one of us is
like a precious tissue which we embroider
as best we know how.

—Anatole France

A RAY OF LIGHT

He who every morning plans the transactions of the day and follows out that plan carries a thread that will guide him through the labyrinth of the most busy life. The orderly arrangement of his time is like a ray of light which darts itself through all his occupations. But where no plan is laid, where disposal of time is surrendered merely to the chance of incidents, chaos will soon reign.

-Victor Hugo

❧ONE DAY AT A TIME❧

THOUGHTS FOR TODAY

-Although I cannot do it all, or do it all perfectly, I will do what I can.

-Good expectations are realistic expectations. Taking things little by little, one step at a time, and one day at a time, leads to positive results.

-I will always try, and if I fail, I will accept it, forgive myself, and try again.

-I need to be patient with myself, just as God is patient with me.

-Living for yesterday or tomorrow is not constructive. Today is what counts.

THIS DAY

Finish every day and be done with it.
You have done what you could. Some
blunders and absurdities no doubt
crept in; forget them as soon as you
can. Tomorrow is a new day; begin it
well and serenely and with too high
a spirit to be cumbered with your old
nonsense. This day is all that is
good and fair. It is too dear, with
its hopes and invitations, to waste
a moment on yesterdays.

—*Ralph Waldo Emerson*

THE BEST

Like the star,
That shines afar,
Without haste
And without rest,
Let each man wheel with steady sway
Round the task that rules the day,
And do his best.
—*Johann Wolfgang von Goethe*

A LIGHTER BURDEN

I compare the troubles which we have
to undergo in the course of the year
to a great bundle of fagots, far too
large for us to lift. But God does
not require us to carry the whole at
once. He mercifully unties the bundle,
and gives us first one stick, which
we are to carry today, and then
another, which we are to carry
tomorrow, and so on. This we might
easily manage, if we would only
take the burden appointed for us
each day; but we choose to increase
our troubles by carrying yesterday's
stick over again today, and adding
tomorrow's burden to our load,
before we are required to bear it.

—*John Newton*

WHAT EACH DAY NEEDS

Would'st shape a noble life? Then cast
No backward glances toward the past,
And though somewhat be lost and gone,
Yet do thou act as one new-born;
What each day needs, that shalt thou ask,
Each day will set its proper tasks.
—*Johann Wolfgang von Goethe*

THE ROAD TO SUCCESS

Throw away all ambition beyond that of doing the day's work well. The travelers on the road to success live in the present, heedless of taking thought for the morrow. Live neither in the past nor in the future, but let each day's work absorb your entire energies...

—*Sir William Osler*

ONE THING AT A TIME

There is no royal road to anything. One thing at a time, and all things in succession. That which grows slowly endures.
—*Josiah Holland*

Anyone can carry his burden, however hard, until nightfall. Anyone can do his work, however hard, for one day.
—*Robert Louis Stevenson*

Be not afraid of going slowly; be afraid only of standing still.
—*Chinese Proverb*

The journey of a thousand miles begins with one step.

—*Lao-Tse*

THE PRESENT

The Present, the Present is all thou hast
For thy sure possessing;
Like the patriarch's angel hold it fast
Till it gives its blessing.
—John Greenleaf Whittier

For yesterday is but a dream,
And tomorrow is only a vision;
But today well lived makes
Every yesterday a dream of happiness,
And every tomorrow a vision of hope.
—from the Sanskrit

The man is happiest who lives from day to day and asks no more, garnering the simple goodness of a life.

—Euripides

Every man's life lies within the present; for the past is spent and done with, and the future is uncertain.

—Marcus Aurelius

There are two days about which nobody should ever worry, and these are yesterday and tomorrow.

—Robert Burdette

Try to be happy in this very present moment; and put off not being so to a time to come...

—Thomas Fuller

PATIENCE IS NEEDED

Patience is needed with everyone, but first of all with ourselves.

—St. Francis de Sales

He that can have patience, can have what he will.

—Benjamin Franklin

There is no great achievement that is not the result of patient working and waiting.

—Josiah Holland

THERE IS NO FAILURE

There is no failure except in no longer
trying. There is no defeat except from
within, no really insurmountable barrier
save our own inherent weakness of
purpose.

—Elbert Hubbard

If at first you don't succeed,
Try, try, try again.

—W. E. Hickson

When you get into a tight place and everything goes against you, 'til it seems as
though you could not hold on a minute
longer, never give up then, for that is just
the place and time that the tide will turn.

—Harriet Beecher Stowe

DON'T QUIT

When things go wrong
   as they sometimes will,
When the road you're
   trudging seems all uphill,
When the funds are low,
   and the debts are high,
And you want to smile,
   but you have to sigh,
When care is pressing
   you down a bit—
Rest if you must,
   but don't you quit.

Success is failure
  turned inside out,
The silver tint of
  the clouds of doubt;
And you never can tell
  how close you are,
It may be near when
  it seems afar.
So, stick to the fight
  when you're hardest hit—
It's when things go wrong
  that you mustn't quit.
                    —*Author Unknown*

❧KEYS TO SERENITY❧

THOUGHTS FOR TODAY

-The secret of serenity is not hindsight or foresight, but insight. When I see things as they are, I know what I can do and I can do it with a tranquil heart.

-The secret of serenity is balance. Keeping a proper perspective, a sense of proportion, and an objective or neutral outlook is essential to keeping my peace of mind.

-The secret of serenity is setting limits. Only by setting limits can I free myself from worry, obsession, overdoing things, dwelling on unimportant details, and agonizing over things I cannot control or change.

-The secret of serenity is staying in touch with myself—and also with God, through prayer and meditation.

THE SERENITY PRAYER

O God, grant us the serenity
to accept what cannot be
changed; the courage to change
what can be changed; and the
wisdom to know one from the
other.

-Reinhold Niebuhr

THE WISDOM OF LIFE

The final wisdom of life requires not the annulment of incongruity but the achievement of serenity within and above it.
—Reinhold Niebuhr

This is moral perfection: to live each day as though it were the last; to be tranquil, sincere, yet not indifferent to one's fate.
—Marcus Aurelius

Nothing can bring you peace but yourself.
—Ralph Waldo Emerson

But the fruit of the Spirit is love, joy, peace, patience, kindness, goodness, faithfulness, gentleness and self-control.
Galatians 5:22,23 (NIV)

THE PATH OF PEACE

To be glad of life, because it gives you the chance to love and to work and to play and to look up at the stars; to be satisfied with your possessions, but not contented with yourself until you have made the best of them; to despise nothing in the world except falsehood and meanness, and to fear nothing except cowardice; to be governed by your admirations rather than by your disgusts; to covet nothing that is your neighbor's except his kindness of heart and gentleness of manners; to think seldom of your enemies, often of your friends and every day of Christ; and to spend as much time as you can with body and with spirit, in God's out-of-doors—these are little guideposts on the footpath of peace.

—*Henry van Dyke*

DO NOT WORRY

"Look at the birds of the air; they do not
sow or reap or store away in barns, and yet
your heavenly Father feeds them. Are you
not much more valuable than they? Who
of you by worrying can add a single hour
to his life?"

Luke 10:26,27 (NIV)

"See how the lilies of the field grow. They
do not labor or spin. Yet I tell you that not
even Solomon in all his splendor was
dressed like one of these."

Luke 10:28,29 (NIV)

"But first seek His kingdom and His righteousness, and all these things will be given to you as well. Therefore do not worry about tomorrow, for tomorrow will worry about itself. Each day has enough trouble of its own."

Luke 10:33,34 (NIV)

ONLY ONE THING IS NEEDED

As Jesus and His disciples were on their way, He came to a village where a woman named Martha opened her home to Him. She had a sister called Mary, who sat at the Lord's feet listening to what He said. But Martha was distracted by all the preparations that had to be made. She came to Him and asked, "Lord, don't you care that my sister has left me to do the work by myself? Tell her to help me!"

"Martha, Martha," the Lord answered, "you are worried and upset about many things, but only one thing is needed. Mary has chosen what is better, and it will not be taken away from her."

Luke 10:38-42 (NIV)

❧JUST FOR TODAY❧

PERSONAL AFFIRMATIONS
BY KATHERINE GARDNER

-Just for today I will try to get a better perspective on my life.

-Just for today I will find the inner strength and courage to live with my inner conflict. I will not expect my recovery to be easy.

-Just for today I will find my happiness within myself, not in anyone else or anything else.

-Just for today I will have the courage to move toward my goals. Fear will not get in my way today.

-Just for today I will not be fair game for the negativity of someone else. I will require respect—and demand respect when necessary.

-Just for today I will figure out what is important and what is not, and this will guide my decisions.

-Just for today I will relinquish grandiose claims to being perfect or perfectly miserable, and be happy with my human life.

-Just for today I will have the strength to risk exposure and individualism.

-Today I will be responsible for my life. I will not judge myself by yesterday's mistakes.

-Just for today I will remember that forgiveness is a giver and resentment is a taker.

-Today I will give myself permission to appreciate myself.

-Today I will give from a full cup, not an empty one. I will give lovingly, but not give all. I will be the center of my own life and belong to myself.

-Just for today I will remember that I am getting better and becoming whole. I will realize that I have more to bring to a relationship than I did yesterday.

-Just for today my life is beautiful, I am beautiful, and I have all that I need to get through the day.

Jacket photograph by
D. Halliman/FPG International
Compiled and edited by Jill Wolf

"Just for Today"
written by Katherine Gardner

"Thoughts for Today"
written by Jill Wolf